SEAFOOD

Recipes from The Cliff

Managing Editor
Melisa Teo

Assistant Editor
Ng Wei Chian

Designer
Yolande Lim

Production Manager
Sin Kam Cheong

First published in 2004 by Archipelago Press
an imprint of Editions Didier Millet
121 Telok Ayer Street
#03-01 Singapore 068590
www.edmbooks.com

For The Cliff
The Sentosa Resort and Spa
2 Bukit Manis Road
Singapore 099891
www.thesentosa.com

© 2004 Editions Didier Millet
Photographs © Jörg Sundermann and
The Sentosa Resort and Spa

ISBN 981-4155-30-6

SEAFOOD

Recipes from The Cliff

Recipes by Shawn Armstrong
Photography by Jörg Sundermann
Text by Don Bosco

ARCHIPELAGO PRESS

CONTENTS

APPETISERS

MAIN COURSES

DESSERTS

BASICS AND GLOSSARY

THE CLIFF

As The Sentosa Resort and Spa's signature restaurant, The Cliff offers an elegant and exciting dining experience in exquisite surroundings. True to its name, diners here are taken to new heights, on account of its physical location, stylish décor, fine cuisine and dedicated team of chefs.

The Cliff is located on prime ground high atop Sentosa Island, surrounded on one side by the luxurious resort facilities of the hotel, and on the other by a wide-open view of the harbour and an endless supply of beautiful sunsets. This dramatic mix of sea, nature and romance is reflected in the interior design, through minimalist lines and the stark textures and surfaces of glass, light, stone and water. At once elegant and comfortable, designer Yashuiro Koichi's style is easily recognisable throughout. The Cliff benefits from his experience and insight, as Koichi remains one of the leading talents in this field, having designed numerous acclaimed restaurants around Japan, Australia, Europe and the Middle East. In turn, guests will not only be greeted by an aesthetic statement, but also have the opportunity to savour the unmistakeable air of distinction and cosmopolitan chic, enhanced by glass pillars and candle displays found on one side of the main entrance walkway. A gentle waterfall on the other side completes the frame of a splendid view of the bay waters beyond. Immediately to one side is an open grill that allows for more creative preparation techniques, while the main kitchen inside remains equipped for more traditional French-style cooking.

This kitchen is a central cooking area surrounded by clear glass walls that strategically open the space to public view. The restaurant is thus rendered at once theatrical and intimate: the chefs are not hidden away behind walls as they go about their preparation, and guests can enjoy witnessing their meal being put together with slick professionalism. This working area has different kitchen stations distinctively outlined, and a team of chefs

> *OPPOSITE: The evocative features of this pavilion-style dining area make it a popular venue for private banquets.*

engrossed in their own respective tasks: making sauces, poaching salmon, finishing the presentation, and so on. With the latest in state-of-the-art equipment and an unhampered workflow, the kitchen is in itself a captivating sight to behold. If anything, guests are quickly convinced that the level of energy and creativity observed here might be hard to match anywhere else.

Just beyond the open kitchen, a set of specially-designed sculptured glass globes mark the start of the main dining area, comprising a series of dining sections that can accommodate 120 guests in all. The main area accommodates a variety of seating preferences, with a set of square tables for a singular dining affair, soft leather lounge chairs around benches which create a more relaxed setting, as well as bench-style tables on a lower platform for casual dining and an excellent survey of the bay area. The well-stocked bar area, too, shares this view of the harbour, which turns into an alluring sight after nightfall when lit up by the glow from ships drifting past in the distance.

Further off into the back are three exclusive dining areas for special functions. The first is a long table under a set of warm lights, perfect for entertaining corporate guests. This connects to a large rectangular table surrounded by tanks of live seafood. Finally, a separate pavilion even further behind houses the most grand table setting yet, with a gentle waterfall on one side and a beautiful view of the South China Sea on the other.

The menu is committed to presenting every single creation with pride. In this aspect, chef de cuisine Shawn Armstrong's personal style and extensive experience is instrumental in defining the restaurant's distinctive character through its food. Every dish is carefully prepared to express a singular vision, with its respective flavours brought together in thoughtful harmony. These are then

> RIGHT: *Clean lines, wooden furnishing and earth-tone upholstery emphasise The Cliff's contemporary style and nature theme.*
> OPPOSITE: *The cosy interior offers stunning views of the sunset.*

complemented with the appropriate garnishes and sauces to ensure a rich, cohesive and satisfying dining experience.

On the whole, the basic ingredients of seafood-based dishes have not changed much over the years: obvious items like lobster and sea bass remain perennial favourites, with freshness the paramount consideration. Certain classics, though, such as the succulent crab cakes, have travelled to The Cliff via Chef Armstrong's journeys over North America, Asia and the Pacific Rim, and continue to please guests in this new setting.

Also of note is the rather inspired pairing of mushrooms and seafood which can be found at The Cliff. Mushrooms are a personal favourite of Armstrong, and different varieties of mushrooms – big and small, light and dark – are harnessed for their varied textures, earthy flavour, and rustic aroma. These are versatile enough to complement the seafood in endlessly creative ways, together with a subtle twist of lemon or orange.

Finally, there's just as much emphasis on presentation, with every dish given an aesthetically attractive appearance that's worthy of its taste. Presentations are comparatively simple, all the better to highlight the individual ingredients and convey the personal style and particular inspiration behind the dish.

For guests looking to use the recipes in this book to replicate some of The Cliff's magical moments at home, Chef Armstrong wishes them the same gratification his team enjoys everyday on the job. "As far as working with seafood goes, you must really care for it," he stresses. "The ingredients don't have to be the most expensive, but they must be the freshest. Then, with a lot of love, a little common sense and just making sure you're organised, you can cook anything."

THE CHEF AS EXPLORER

Everyday on the job, chefs at The Cliff are reminded to consider themselves as culinary explorers, guided by their sense of taste, touch, smell and sight, as well as their experience and common sense. Recipes are employed like maps to get them from one point to another, but it is the passion they muster in the kitchen that makes all the difference.

This advice stems from the personal philosophy of Shawn Armstrong, who became The Cliff's chef de cuisine at the age of 30 – a young chef by his own reckoning, but who is by no means lacking in professional experience. Prior to this appointment, the Texan had proven his mettle in a number of leading seafood specialty restaurants around the world, over a career that has spanned American establishment McCormick and Schmick's Seafood Restaurant, Hong Kong's Oyster and Wine Bar, and the Maldives' luxury resort Taj Coral Reef.

Chef Armstrong inherited his passion for good food from his tightly-knit family, particularly his grandparents who were always enthusiastic about putting together festive feasts. As a boy, he quickly learnt to appreciate all the different tastes, flavours, sounds and smells of the kitchen, and the endless opportunities to be creative. He recalls: "Two of the things I love most are American football and cooking. I've got a big family that would get together for the weekend, or celebrations like the Fourth of July, Thanksgiving, or Christmas. My time was always split between being with the ladies in the kitchen, and the men watching the big football game. And more often than not, actually, I ended up in the kitchen, keeping my ears on the football game."

After college, he entertained a brief diversion as a firefighter, but decided to commit to a culinary career and enrolled in the School of Culinary Arts in Houston, Texas in 1997. "I did it a little

> ABOVE: *Chef Armstrong presides over The Cliff's immaculate kitchen.*
> RIGHT: *His classical French culinary training is immediately apparent in the way each dish is painstakingly prepared and presented.*
> OPPOSITE: *The Cliff's open kitchen brings together state-of-the-art equipment with some of the region's most inspired talents.*

all the different creatures that can come out of the sea, Chef Armstrong constantly encounters new species that he has never seen before, and finds an endless supply of ingredients to pique his interest. And, as with the rowdiness of competitive sports, Chef Armstrong finds the flow of activity in the kitchen extremely energising. The ideal reward for a good day's work? "On some days when you've cooked some really nice food and everyone's happy, you feel like you're standing on top of a mountain," he offers with no hesitation. Which pretty much explains why this man is right at home at The Cliff.

differently compared to most people," he muses. "I wasn't the classic stereotype of a chef, peeling potatoes when I was 14 or 15 years old and slowly working my way up the ranks. I went to culinary school after getting experience in a restaurant for a while, and that decision paid off by taking my skills and techniques to a much higher level."

Given his formal education in French culinary techniques, his experience at The Cliff has allowed him to develop his own approach in matching traditional techniques with regional ingredients, without straying into fusion territory. "I try to cook in a contemporary French style, based heavily on seafood," he explains, "but most of all, to have a good time while I'm doing it." His preferred flavours reflect a seasonal range, depending on the places from which his ingredients are imported, and his team of chefs equally share this attention to geographical and cultural authenticity.

Even after close to a decade spent in the kitchen, seafood still excites him because there is so much variety to work with. With

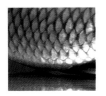

SPLENDOURS OF THE SEA

LIVELY ENCOUNTERS

It is little wonder that seafood continues to grow in popularity with epicures around the world. Generally high in nutritional value and rich in minerals and calcium while low in sodium, it is touted by medical authorities as a healthy alternative to red meat. Meanwhile, leading chefs all around the world have been successfully experimenting with and refining their preparation styles, and the overall quality and variety of supplies have also improved tremendously, thanks to better harvesting and shipping methods.

When picking out whole fish, there are a number of signs to look out for that indicate freshness, the most obvious being the eyes. If it's a fresh catch, the eyes will still be full and clear, sometimes even bulging a little. Murky, pinkish eyes reveal that the fish has lost its freshness. The gills should also have a reddish tint. This loses its vividness over time and will turn brown or green.

> *ABOVE: When choosing fish, check that the flesh is not broken, the scales are intact, and the skin has not lost its shine.*
> *RIGHT: Fresh tiger prawns should be meaty, slightly salty and crisp.*
> *OPPOSITE: The extra lengths one is required to go to in order to store, handle and serve caviar are worth the rare treat.*

Some people prefer to press the flesh with their fingers as another method to detect freshness. Fresh fish remain firm to the touch, but will gradually lose their texture until the flesh even starts to slip readily off the bones. Another good indication of freshness is a shiny skin and intact scales. All fish naturally lose both their markings and scales, as well as develop a slimy feel the longer they have left the water.

Likewise, fillets should look freshly cut, slightly translucent, and show no brownish discolouration along the edges. The flesh should be elastic, firm to the touch, and should not break apart easily. Make sure the fillets you buy don't come packed with excess water, as this will make them deteriorate even faster.

Fresh shellfish should not be anything more than mildly and pleasantly aromatic, similar to seaweed. The shells should appear moist, and not show any cracks. Live clams, oysters, and mussels should keep their shells clammed tight, or at least respond to your touch by closing quickly. If shucked, the meat should be full and still covered with a clear or slightly milky liquor.

Check for active leg movements when observing live lobsters and crabs, though they might be sluggish if kept in refrigeration. With the exception of soft-shell crabs, the shells should always remain hard. When picked up, lobsters should instinctively curl their tails under the body, and not hold them hanging down.

Fresh raw shrimp will have translucent shells and firm flesh ranging from grey to pink in colour, depending on the variety. Black spots are a clear indication of deterioration. Whole squid should retain their clear eyes and layer of skin, and the flesh should be firm. Over time, the skin will tear and turn pinkish.

As a general guide, fresh seafood should always be kept as close to 0°C as possible. Home cooks should set the freezer to the lowest setting at least two hours in advance, and not pack in too much as the freezer will then be less effective. The back of the lower shelf is often the coldest section, and remains the best place to store seafood. Seafood is ideally consumed within two days of purchase, except for live lobsters and crabs which should be cooked on the very same day.

When thawing frozen fish, it is better to let it defrost gradually in the refrigerator or microwave oven than leaving it at room

temperature. This is to minimise losing the liquid that comes off the fish as it thaws. Also known as the 'drip', this liquid contains a significant amount of proteins and minerals derived from the fish, and is thus high in nutritional content.

FRESH CUTS

To fillet a fish, lay it on a cutting board and make a slit sideways all the way along the back. The slit should start from the tail and end at the head, and be deep enough to separate the top fillet from the backbone.

Next, make one cut at the tail and another just behind the head, which will then allow the top fillet to be lifted away smoothly. Remove the head and backbone, and clean the bottom fillet of any remaining bones. Each fillet may then be further separated into two, if there is a row of bones along the middle to remove.

Shrimp can be easily deveined with a sharp knife, cold water, and a bit of practice. Start with a small cut along the back of the shrimp, which will allow the prominent dark vein to be pulled out. Throw this away, then rinse the shrimp in cold water to remove any extra grit. If the shrimps are small, or the vein isn't dark, deveining might be neither necessary nor worth the effort.

Lobsters and crabs must always be boiled live, as the meat begins to decompose and deteriorate immediately once they die. Before cooking a lobster, lift it up to make sure the legs and tail are still moving. The most common and easiest cooking method is to grip the lobster behind the head and quickly lower it into boiling water. When cooked, its antennae should pull away with ease. Similarly, crabs should be quickly cleaned and boiled in water that has been seasoned with salt.

> ABOVE: Any fish can be quickly filleted with a basic understanding of its bone structure and a sharp knife.
> OPPOSITE: The preparation possibilities and health benefits of fresh salmon make it a prized ingredient among chefs.

These days, mussels are largely obtained from special farms and come pre-cleaned. They simply need to be washed, and have their byssal threads (hair-like protrusions from the shell) removed. Always keep caviar in the refrigerator until just prior to serving, and handle carefully so as not to crush the eggs. Use a mother-of-pearl caviar spoon, as sterling silver will both impart a metallic taste, as well as end up being stained by the caviar.

A FEAST BECKONS

How one approaches cooking a fish will depend on the type of flesh and natural flavour, as well as its texture. White flesh that is tender and flaky, such as cod and yellowtail snapper, should be steamed, baked, poached or sautéed, while those with a stronger flavour, such as wolffish and rock sole, will be better deep-fried. If it has a much firmer texture – such as grouper, white sea bass and red snapper – you can consider grilling.

Darker meat such as monkfish, pink salmon, striped bass and eel are more commonly steamed, poached, baked, grilled or sautéed; in addition, the firmer varieties such as black sea bass, tuna, shark and swordfish are especially good for pickling.

Lobsters and crabs are most often steamed, baked or sautéed, while shrimp can be grilled, steamed, deep-fried or baked. Oysters, clams and scallops are actually quite versatile, and can be steamed, stewed, deep-fried, baked, or even cooked in a microwave oven and yet retain their natural flavour.

Langoustines, also known as Dublin Bay prawns, can be cooked in salt water or a spicy stock, but can be savoured just as well steamed, grilled or coated with butter and fried. Be sure to remove the shell and intestinal canal first.

On the other hand, some seafood can be eaten raw, though there are very strict conditions to be observed. The best example is probably Japanese sashimi, a popular delicacy consisting of thin slices of raw seafood which are enjoyed with wasabi and a

quick dip in soya sauce. Despite the minimal preparation, one can nonetheless expect to encounter a wide range of flavours here even without seasoning or cooking, from the subtle taste of red snapper to the characteristically fishy mackerel. A culinary adventure in this instance would be to sample the fugu, otherwise known as the notoriously poisonous blowfish. Unless it is prepared just right, the flesh will impart enough poison to shut down a human being's central nervous system in the blink of an eye. Even today, this fish remains a highly prized, and significantly pricey, delicacy.

While there are many other varieties of sashimi to choose from – including salmon, tuna, prawn and octopus – sashimi must only be prepared from the freshest of supplies, and even then strictly from saltwater sources. Freshwater fish tend to carry parasites that are killed during cooking, while saltwater fish are free from them and might thus be safely eaten raw.

Similarly, ceviche, a popular South American dish, comprises raw seafood – such as fish, shrimp or lobster – left to stew in acidic citrus juices. Traditionally, fishermen would use darker fish such as black sea bass, and soak this in lemon or lime juice and a variety of seasonings. Left to sit, the chemical reaction eventually changes the colour of the flesh and makes it appear cooked.

Always investigate the source of your seafood if you intend to serve it raw, and only purchase from established suppliers who know how to store and handle them properly. Raw oysters require particular attention. Unless they are properly refrigerated throughout, a poisonous bacterium (Vibrio vulnificus) will develop in them to levels unsafe for the human body.

People with health risks – those suffering from diabetes, for example, or liver and kidney problems – should generally avoid all forms of raw shellfish unless their doctor advises otherwise.

> *ABOVE: Champagne remains the drink of choice when pairing with seafood.*
> *RIGHT: Lobsters are a delicious option for stylish home entertaining.*
> *OPPOSITE: Diners are invariably drawn to the dramatic marine hues of The Cliff's wine display.*

tantalising tray of poached fish, and in every style from French to Japanese. On the whole, dishes with a light, acidic sauce are better paired with a citrus-flavoured Champagne, while the dishes with richer sauces go better with a full-bodied Champagne.

These are but a few of the myriad culinary possibilities in the continued exploration and appreciation of seafood dishes. We trust that the following recipes will find you well-fed and satisfied on this exciting journey.

WINE NOTES

When pairing with wines, one can aspire to master the wide range of available options and combinations through the sound recommendations of a friendly connoisseur, coupled with the benefit of personal experience. In general, seafood and wine pairings are appreciated on the basis of how the aroma and flavour of one complements or contrasts with the other. Full-bodied white wines like the top-quality Bordeaux or Chardonnay are often selected for most seafood, with the exception of spicy dishes, while the lighter, fruity red wines can also work if the seafood dishes aren't particularly rich or oily.

The conventional opinion is that any good wine will be wasted on dishes with overpowering flavours, such as curries. In such cases, try choosing something cool and light, perhaps even fruity, to provide a refreshing counterpoint.

Champagne, though, deserves a special mention. While it is traditionally offered alongside raw oysters, caviar and salmon, and otherwise reserved for certain celebratory occasions, it effectively complements a wider variety of seafood dishes, whether a rich lobster feast, hearty calamari platter, or a

THREE WAYS WITH OYSTERS (TEMPURA OF OYSTERS AND OYSTERS WITH CUCUMBER JELLY AND CHAMPAGNE MIGNONETTE)

Serves 6

3 to 4 shallots, finely minced
1 tbsp freshly cracked black pepper
50 ml Champagne
50 ml Champagne vinegar
4 Japanese cucumbers, chopped
9 sheets gelatine, soaked in iced water
Salt to taste
1 drop green food colouring (optional)
1 small fennel bulb
2 tsp orange juice
1 tbsp extra virgin olive oil
2 tsp white wine vinegar
Pepper to taste
2 tbsp tempura flour
50 ml cold soda water
½ tsp sesame oil
½ tbsp white sesame seeds
18 oysters, shucked (see Basics)
500 ml oil for deep-frying
50 ml wasabi aioli (see Basics)
1 tsp black sesame seeds
30 g salmon roe (optional)
6 sprigs flat-leaf parsley
1 kg rock salt (optional)

> To prepare the **Champagne mignonette**, mix the shallots, pepper, Champagne and vinegar, and chill.
> To prepare the **cucumber jelly**, purée the cucumber in a food processor and strain through a fine-mesh sieve. Discard the pulp and strain the juice through a damp cheesecloth to remove all sediments. If needed, add water to juice to make 500 ml.
> Strain the gelatine and combine with the cucumber juice in a pot. Bring to a simmer, add the salt and remove from heat once the salt and gelatine has dissolved. Add the food colouring and mix well. Pour the mixture into a 20-by-10-cm shallow pan and keep refrigerated until the gelatine sets.
> To prepare the fennel salad, remove the fennel's fronds and reserve for garnishing. Using a sharp knife, slice the fennel bulb thinly. Combine it with the orange juice, olive oil and white wine vinegar in a mixing bowl and toss well. Season to taste.
> Combine the **tempura** flour, soda water, sesame oil and seeds and salt in a mixing bowl and whisk until smooth. Keep refrigerated until required.
> Dip 6 oysters into the batter and deep-fry the oysters in batches until golden. Remove from oil and drain on kitchen paper.
> Place each fried oyster in a clean shell and top with wasabi aioli and black sesame seeds.
> Place ½ tbsp of fennel salad in each of 6 empty shells, then top with an oyster. Garnish with diced cucumber jelly, salmon roe and fennel frond.
> Garnish the remaining 6 oysters with Champagne mignonette and parsley sprigs.
> Divide the rock salt (to keep the oysters from sliding around and tipping over) among 6 plates and place each type of oyster on every plate.

CRAB CAKES WITH PAPAYA CEVICHE

> To prepare the **papaya ceviche**, combine the jicama, papaya, capsicum, red onion, ½ tbsp of chopped coriander, chilli and lime juice in a bowl and mix well. Keep chilled until required.
> Check the cooked crabmeat for shells and lightly press out any excess water.
> To prepare the **crab cakes**, combine the onions, mixed capsicums, egg, remaining chopped coriander, mayonnaise, Tabasco sauce, lemon juice and mustard in a bowl and mix well. Season with salt and pepper, and gently fold in the crabmeat, taking care not to break the meat up. Fold in half the breadcrumbs. Refrigerate the mixture for 20 minutes.
> Divide the mixture into 10 portions, using your hands to shape them into patties. Dredge the patties in the remaining breadcrumbs.
> Heat oil in a pan and pan-fry the crab cakes on each side for 2 minutes over medium heat until golden brown.
> Top the crab cakes with the chilled papaya ceviche and garnish with coriander sprigs.

Serves 5

75 g jicama, diced
100 g ripe papaya, diced
25 g red capsicum, diced
1 tbsp diced red onion
1½ tbsp chopped coriander
½ bird's eye chilli, minced
25 ml lime juice
450 g white crabmeat, cooked
2 tbsp diced onions
3 tbsp diced mixed (yellow, green and red) capsicums
1 egg
4 tbsp mayonnaise
1 tbsp Tabasco sauce
Juice from 1 lemon
1 tbsp Dijon mustard
Salt and pepper to taste
200 g breadcrumbs
4 tbsp oil
5 to 10 sprigs coriander

Oyster and Artichoke Bisque

> Reserve the **oyster** juices. Heat the butter in a pot, add the celery, leek and shallot and sauté until translucent. Add the garlic and 6 oysters with reserved juices, and sauté until the edges of the oysters begin to curl. Add the Pernod and reduce until almost dry. Sprinkle the flour over and stir until well mixed. Add the stock and stir until the flour is completely dissolved. Add the **artichokes** and simmer for 20 minutes. Add the spinach leaves and cook for a further 10 minutes.

> To prepare the **bisque**, purée this mixture in a food processor, then strain through a fine-mesh sieve.

> Return the purée to the heat and bring to a simmer, stirring constantly to prevent burning. Add the cream, mix well and season with salt and pepper.

> In lightly salted water, gently poach the remaining oysters until their edges begin to curl, then remove and drain.

> Divide the soup and poached oysters among 4 bowls, top oysters with crème fraîche and caviar, and garnish with dill sprigs.

18 fresh oysters, shucked (see Basics)
25 g butter
2 tbsp diced celery
2 tbsp diced leek (white part only)
1 shallot, peeled and diced
1 garlic, peeled and minced
20 ml Pernod
1½ tsp flour, sifted
250 ml fish stock (see Basics)
200 g canned artichokes
Handful of spinach leaves
35 ml whipping cream
Salt and white pepper to taste
50 g crème fraîche
50 g Beluga caviar
12 (2.5-cm) sprigs dill

Serves 4

CUCUMBER GAZPACHO AND TIAN OF CRABMEAT
WITH PINK GRAPEFRUIT VINAIGRETTE

Serves 4

500 g Japanese cucumber, chopped
    (reserve 4 tsp, cut into short sticks,
    for garnishing)
100 g celery, chopped
40 g green capsicum, seeds removed
    and chopped
4 sprigs flat-leaf parsley, chopped
15 g chives, chopped
25 g mint, chopped
10 basil leaves, chopped
1 garlic clove, peeled and chopped
75 ml olive oil
120 ml white wine vinegar
100 ml water
250 g ice
Salt and pepper to taste
1 pink grapefruit, peeled, with pith and
    seeds removed
½ tsp castor sugar
50 ml corn oil
140 g king crabmeat, shredded
Flesh from 2 avocados, diced
6 tbsp crème fraîche
4 sprigs shiso cress
1 tsp salmon roe
4 herbed bread crisps

> To prepare the **cucumber gazpacho**, combine the chopped cucumber, celery, capsicum, parsley, chives, mint, basil leaves, garlic, olive oil, 75 ml of white wine vinegar, water, ice, salt and pepper in a food processor and blend until smooth.
> Working over a bowl to catch all the juice, shred the grapefruit pulp and squeeze out the juice.
> To prepare the **pink grapefruit vinaigrette**, combine the pulp, juice, castor sugar and remaining white wine vinegar, whisk in the corn oil and season with salt and pepper.
> Toss the crabmeat and half the grapefruit vinaigrette together in a bowl.
> Toss the diced avocado and remaining vinaigrette in a second bowl. Season each with salt and pepper.
> To prepare the **tian of crabmeat**, place a ring mould in the centre of a soup plate, and fill half of it with avocado. Press the avocado in firmly, then pack the top half with crabmeat, pressing firmly again. Use a palette knife to spread a smooth layer of crème fraîche on the crabmeat. Carefully remove the mould.
> Garnish the crabmeat tower with cucumber sticks, shiso cress, salmon roe and herbed bread crisps. Ladle gazpacho around to serve.

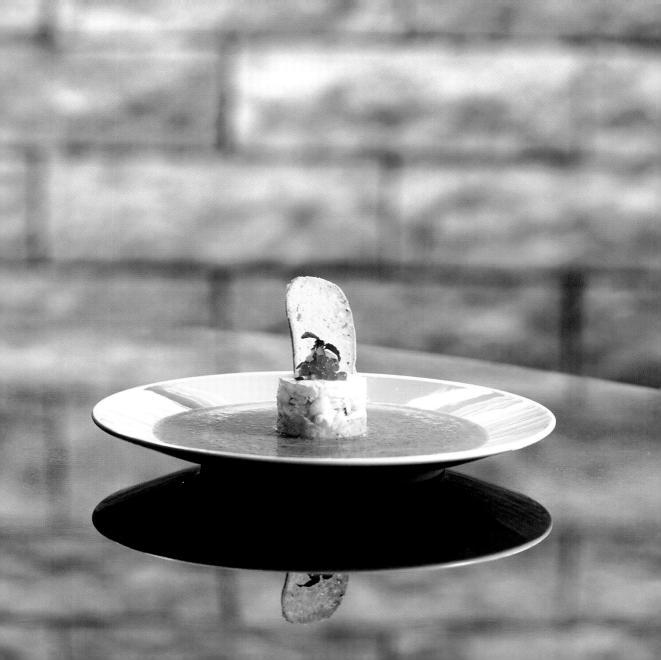

Torchon of Marinated Foie Gras with Ice Wine Aspic

Serves 12

1 pc (about 500 g) raw foie gras
1 tbsp sea salt
½ tbsp freshly cracked white pepper
375 ml ice wine or late harvest sweet
   white wine
7 gelatine sheets, soaked in cold water
255 ml mirin
100 g raisins
3 L chicken stock (see Basics)
500 ml balsamic vinegar
1 loaf brioche or baguette, sliced thinly
   and toasted

> Leave the foie gras out at room temperature for about 1 to 2 hours until it is soft and pliable.

> Using your hands, carefully separate the 2 lobes that make up the liver, then use the point of a sharp knife to remove as many veins (the veins run in a 'Y' shape down the lobe) as possible, taking care not to break the lobes or overwork them till they become too soft.

> To prepare the **marinated foie gras**, season the liver generously with salt and pepper, then sprinkle the remaining mirin over. Marinate the liver overnight.

> To prepare the **ice wine aspic**, bring the ice wine to a slow boil. Remove the gelatine sheets from the

water and gently wring them to remove excess water. Add to the ice wine and stir until the gelatine dissolves completely. Remove from heat and pour the mixture into a wide shallow container and chill for about 2 hours to set.

> Reduce 150 ml of the mirin by half then add the raisins and cook until the sauce is syrupy. Mix in 25 ml of mirin and remove from heat.

> To prepare the **torchon**, use a damp but clean cheesecloth or dish towel to roll the liver tightly into a cylinder, twisting the ends to compact the liver. Secure the ends tightly with butcher string.

> Bring the stock to a simmer. Poach the torchon in it for 8 minutes, then submerge it in an ice bath. Hang the torchon vertically in your refrigerator overnight for optimum results.

> Reduce the balsamic vinegar over medium heat to a glaze and allow to cool.

> Unwrap the torchon and use a thin sharp knife dipped in hot water to cut it into 1-cm-thick slices. Drizzle the balsamic glaze on serving plates, arrange a few slices of torchon on each plate and garnish with diced ice wine aspic, raisins and toast.

Seared spice-crusted tuna with tamarind and onion relish

> To prepare the **tamarind and onion relish**, use a fork to break up the tamarind pulp. Remove and discard the seeds.
> Purée the pulp, soy sauce, 2 tbsp of balsamic vinegar and sugar in a food processor for 15 seconds. Strain the mixture through a fine-mesh sieve, discard the pulp and reserve the liquid.
> Mix in the onions and whisk in the sesame oil and 3 tbsp of olive oil.
> Grind the peppercorns and allspice together using a spice grinder, coffee grinder or mortar and pestle.
> To prepare the **seared spice-crusted tuna**, season the tuna with sea salt, then coat the top and bottom of the tuna with the spice mixture.
> Heat the oil in a pan until it begins to smoke, then gently sear one coated side of the tuna for about 20 seconds. Turn over and sear the other coated side for 20 seconds. Remove from pan and set aside.
> Combine the rocket leaves, the remaining balsamic vinegar and olive oil, salt and pepper in a mixing bowl and toss well.
> Slice the tuna lengthwise as thinly as possible (about 0.4 or 0.5 cm thick). You should get about 6 slices out of each tuna loin. Roll up the slices as shown.
> Spoon some tamarind and onion relish onto each plate and top with the tuna rolls. Garnish the tuna with sea salt, rocket leaves, pine nuts and shiso cress. Sprinkle some of the remaining spice mixture on the plates.

Serves 4

1 tbsp tamarind pulp, soaked in 3 tbsp hot water for 15 minutes
2½ tbsp soy sauce
2⅓ tbsp balsamic vinegar
½ tbsp sugar
½ onion, peeled and finely minced
1 tsp sesame oil
4 tbsp olive oil
4 tbsp Sichuan peppercorns, toasted
1 tbsp black peppercorns, toasted
2 tbsp allspice
4 tuna loins, trimmed into 10-by-2.5-by-2.5-cm pieces
Sea salt to taste
1 tbsp oil for frying
40 g rocket leaves
Salt and pepper to taste
1 tbsp pine nuts, toasted
8 to12 sprigs shiso cress

Shaved Asparagus Salad with Mascarpone and Tomato Confit

> Preheat oven to 100°C. To prepare the **tomato confit**, blanch the tomatoes and refresh in iced water immediately. Peel, then cut them in half. Remove the seeds and pulp, then brush the tomato flesh with olive oil and season with castor sugar and salt.

> Place them with their cut sides down on a baking tray lined with greaseproof paper. Sprinkle the garlic slices and chopped thyme over and bake for 2 to 2½ hours, basting periodically with olive oil, until the tomatoes become flat and glossy.

> To prepare the **Parmesan crisp**, sift together the flour, baking powder and a pinch of salt. In an electric mixer fixed with a dough hook, combine this with the butter, a pinch of sugar, milk, egg yolk and 40 g of Parmesan. Mix until the dough is smooth, then remove it from the mixer and knead it by hand on a floured surface for 5 minutes. Let the dough rest for 20 minutes.

> Preheat oven to 180°C. Roll out the dough evenly (about 0.3 cm thick) and cut it into thin triangular wedges. Chill these for 30 minutes, then bake them for 5 to 8 minutes until golden and crisp.

> In a mixing bowl, combine the **mascarpone** and truffle oil. Season with salt and mix well.

> Over medium heat, reduce the balsamic vinegar to a syrup-like consistency. Using a small paintbrush, paint this on 4 plates.

> To prepare the **shaved asparagus salad**, season the asparagus with salt and pepper, toss in sherry vinegar and olive oil.

> Arrange 2 pieces of tomato confit on each plate. Top with the shaved asparagus salad, followed by 1 tbsp of mascarpone. Sprinkle the remaining grated Parmesan over. Garnish with a sprinkling of ground black pepper and a Parmesan crisp.

Serves 4

4 ripe tomatoes
100 ml extra virgin olive oil (set 2 tbsp aside for the asparagus)
1 tbsp castor sugar
Salt to taste
2 cloves garlic, peeled and thinly sliced
Leaves from 4 sprigs thyme, coarsely chopped
100 g plain flour
¼ tsp baking powder
25 g butter
1½ tbsp milk
1 egg yolk
90 g grated Parmesan
100 g mascarpone
1 tsp truffle oil
250 ml balsamic vinegar
12 asparagus spears, blanched then dipped in ice bath, tips and bottoms removed
1 tbsp sherry vinegar
Freshly ground black pepper

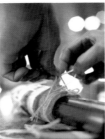

CAESAR SALAD WITH CAJUN PRAWNS, QUAIL EGG AND MARINATED ANCHOVIES

> To prepare the **salad dressing**, purée the anchovies, mustard, garlic, Worcestershire sauce, vinegar, lemon juice, Parmesan, egg yolk, salt and pepper in a food processor until smooth. Reduce speed and slowly incorporate the olive oil until the mixture emulsifies.

> To prepare the **Cajun spice mix**, pound the peppercorns, cumin and mustard seeds using a mortar and pestle (or food processor) to obtain a powder. Mix this with the paprika, chilli powder, thyme, garlic and onion powder, and sea salt.

> To prepare the **bread ring**, remove the contents, label, top and bottom of a cylindrical tin can and wash thoroughly. Cut the bread into rectangular pieces measuring 0.5 cm thick, 3.5 cm wide and long enough to wrap the bread around the can with the ends just overlapping. Grease the outside of the can and wrap a strip of bread around. Secure it with butcher string and deep-fry in oil over medium heat until the bread is golden brown. Remove from oil and drain on kitchen paper. When cool enough to handle, carefully remove the string. Prepare 5 rings.

> Preheat oven to 160°C. Place the pancetta on a baking tray lined with greaseproof paper and bake for 15 minutes until crisp.

> Boil the **quail eggs** for 2 minutes 15 seconds. Cool in ice bath. Peel.

> To prepare the **Cajun prawns**, heat 2 tbsp of oil in a pan, dust the prawns with Cajun spice, then pan-fry them over high heat for about 2 minutes on each side, turning over once.

> To prepare the **Caesar salad**, toss the lettuce in the dressing. Place 1 bread ring on a plate and fill the ring with lettuce and prawns. Garnish with Parmesan and arrange the quail eggs, pancetta and **marinated anchovies** on the side. Sprinkle with black pepper.

Serves 5

340 g tinned anchovies
1 tsp yellow mustard
1 garlic clove, peeled and minced
Dash of Worcestershire sauce
25 ml red wine vinegar
Few drops of lemon juice
25 g grated Parmesan
1 egg yolk
Salt to taste
½ tsp freshly grounded black pepper
125 ml olive oil
2 tsp black peppercorns, toasted
2 tsp cumin seeds, toasted
2 tsp mustard seeds, toasted
2 tbsp paprika
2 tsp chilli powder
2 tbsp dried thyme (or oregano)
2 tsp garlic powder
1 tbsp onion powder
2 tsp sea salt
5 pcs foccacia (or ciabatta), frozen
Oil for deep-frying
5 thin slices pancetta
5 quail eggs
10 prawns, shells removed, tails intact
100 to 150 g baby romaine lettuce
50 g Parmesan shavings
5 pre-marinated white anchovies

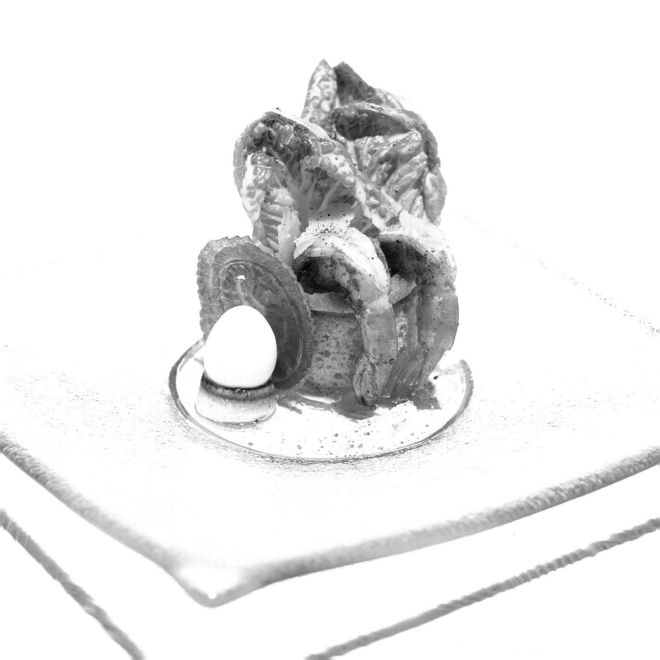

ASIAN GRAVLAX WITH WASABI AIOLI

Serves 10 to 15

250 g grated palm sugar
250 g sea salt
2 tbsp Sichuan peppercorns
2 tbsp white peppercorns
1 (about 1.5 kg) salmon fillet, with skin on
20 g coriander leaves and stems
2 stalks lemon grass, split lengthwise
3 tsp wasabi powder
1 egg yolk
½ tbsp lemon juice
1½ tbsp rice wine vinegar
1 tbsp soy sauce
2 tsp Dijon mustard
½ tbsp mirin
Salt and pepper to taste
250 ml canola oil
100 to 150 g tatsoi leaves
75 ml lemon vinaigrette (mix 1 part lemon
   juice with 3 parts extra virgin olive oil)
2 tbsp black sesame seeds

> To prepare the **Asian gravlax**, combine the palm sugar, salt and peppercorns in a bowl. Cut the salmon fillet in half. Place one half of the salmon, skin side down, on a large plate and cover it with half the sugar-salt mixture. Place the coriander and lemon grass on the salmon, then cover with the remaining sugar-salt mixture and top with the other salmon half, flesh side down.
> Leave at room temperature for 3 hours then refrigerate for 48 hours, turning the salmon over once and basting frequently with the curing mixture.
> To prepare the **wasabi aioli**, purée the wasabi powder, egg yolk, lemon juice, rice wine vinegar, soy sauce, mustard, mirin, salt and pepper in a food processor set on low speed and slowly incorporate oil until well mixed.
> Using a thin sharp knife, separate the salmon flesh from the skin, then slice the flesh as thinly as possible.
> Arrange the salmon slices on several plates or a serving platter with tatsoi tossed in lemon vinaigrette on top. Drizzle wasabi aioli over and garnish with sesame seeds. (This is a perfect dish for large parties as it is easy to prepare and can be done well in advance. Traditional accompaniments for the dish are mustard and savoury biscuits.)

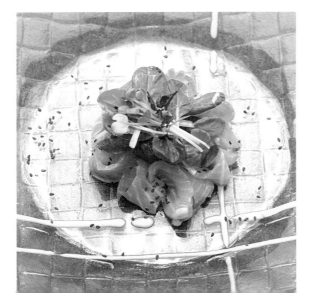

FENNEL TARTE TATIN WITH HONEY GLAZED SCALLOPS

> To prepare the **fennel tarte Tatin**, combine the fennel, milk, garlic, onion, peppercorns, bay leaf, ½ tbsp of honey and ¼ tbsp of salt in a pot. Bring to a simmer for 10 minutes until fennel is cooked but still firm. Remove the fennel and rinse. Trim off a quarter of the bottom portion and discard.

> Place the fennel cut side down in a shallow pan and add the thyme. Add wine and reduce until dry and the fennel begins to caramelise. Add 2 tbsp of honey and caramelise the fennel, on their cut sides only.

> Grease 4 small round aluminium tart trays. Divide 1 tbsp of honey among the 4 trays. Place the fennel bulbs cut side down in the trays, then press the puff pastry evenly on top of the fennel.

> Beat 1 egg and brush the puff pastry with it. Refrigerate the pastry for at least 20 minutes. Boil the other egg for 4 minutes. Cool in ice bath and peel.

> To prepare the **sauce**, blanch the lettuce leaf in chicken stock for 15 to 20 seconds until just wilted. Refresh in ice bath. Cool the stock and combine it with the lettuce leaf, egg, 50 to 75 g of fennel trimmings from above and olive oil, then purée in a food processor until smooth. Strain through a fine-mesh sieve and discard pulp. Add Pernod and adjust seasoning. Keep chilled.

> Preheat oven to 180°C. Bake the tart for 10 to 12 minutes until the pastry is golden.

> To prepare the **honey glazed scallops**, heat oil in a non-stick pan until it begins to smoke. Season scallops with salt and pepper, then sauté each side for 45 seconds. Working quickly, baste both sides with the remaining honey.

> Whisk or blend the cold sauce until foamy. Place 3 scallops in the centre of a plate, top with the warm tart, spoon sauce over and garnish with dill.

Serves 4

4 small young fennel bulbs, fronds trimmed
   and veins removed
700 ml milk (enough to cover the fennel bulbs)
2 garlic cloves, peeled and minced
½ onion, peeled and chopped
½ tsp black peppercorns
1 bay leaf
5½ tbsp honey
Salt and pepper to taste
1 sprig thyme
400 ml dry white wine
Non-stick cooking spray or butter for greasing
4 sheets puff pastry (each 0.1 cm thick and
   6 cm in diameter)
2 eggs
1 romaine lettuce leaf
50 ml chicken stock (see Basics)
25 ml olive oil
½ tbsp Pernod
1 tbsp oil for frying
12 large sea scallops, shells removed
4 sprigs dill

PAN-ROASTED CRAYFISH AND SEARED FOIE GRAS
ON CORN MUFFIN WITH ORANGE MARMALADE

> Purée 200 g of **corn** kernels with the water in a food processor until smooth. Strain through a fine-mesh sieve, gently pressing the solids with a spoon to extract more liquid. Discard the pulp and bring the corn juice to a simmer over moderate heat, without boiling (or the corn juice will curdle). Stir constantly until the mixture is thick enough to coat the back of a spoon. Set aside.

> Heat the butter and olive oil in another pan, add carrots, celery, shallots and soy beans, then sauté over medium heat for 1 minute. Add thyme, the remaining corn kernels and thickened corn purée. Season with salt and pepper.

> Reheat the **corn muffins** in the oven. Cut them in half and spread a layer of **orange marmalade** on each muffin.

> To prepare the **pan-roasted crayfish**, season the crayfish meat with sea salt and ground black pepper. Heat the duck fat in a non-stick pan. Sauté the meat from the crayfish tail on each side for 3 minutes over medium heat. Add the claw meat to the pan and sauté for 1 minute on each side. Remove, set aside and keep warm.

> To prepare the **seared foie gras**, heat a pan over medium-high heat and sear the foie gras for about 1 minute on each side. After cooking, season with sea salt and pepper.

> Heat the crayfish sauce and spoon a pool of it into the centre of a plate. Top it with corn and a corn muffin. Place a piece of crayfish on the muffin and top it with a piece of foie gras.

500 g fresh corn kernels (about 5 ears of corn)
100 ml water
1 tbsp butter
½ tbsp olive oil
1 tbsp finely diced carrots
1 tbsp finely diced celery
1 tbsp finely diced shallots
200 g shelled soy beans
½ tsp chopped thyme leaves
Salt and pepper to taste
4 corn muffins (see Basics)
4 tbsp orange marmalade (see Basics)
4 (each about 300 g) crayfish, boiled and
  shells removed
2 tbsp duck fat or oil
4 pcs (each about 60 g and 1 to 1.5 cm thick)
  raw foie gras, veins and fat trimmed
Sea salt to taste
200 ml crayfish sauce (see Basics)

Serves 4

MEDALLIONS OF MONKFISH WRAPPED IN PARMA HAM
WITH BRAISED LAMB SHANK IN CABBAGE PARCEL

> To prepare the **braised lamb shank**, season the lamb shanks with salt and pepper. Heat the oil in a large, heavy-bottom pot and brown the lamb shanks evenly.

> Preheat oven to 180°C. Remove the lamb shanks from the pot and add the carrot, onion and celery to the same pot. Caramelise the vegetables, then return the lamb shanks to the pot. Add the parsley stems, tomato sauce, brown stock and wine. Ensure that the lamb shanks are submerged at least halfway and bring to a boil. Cover the pot tightly with aluminium foil and transfer it to the oven. Let the mixture cook in the oven for 1½ hours until the meat is almost falling off the bone, then remove from heat.

> Remove the lamb shanks from the liquid. Reduce the liquid over medium heat until it achieves the consistency of a rich sauce. Strain and set aside.

> Once the lamb shanks are cool enough to handle, remove the meat from the bones and shred it with your hands. Season the shredded lamb with salt and pepper and mix with 120 ml of the braising sauce.

> To prepare the **cabbage parcels**, line a small bowl with 2 cabbage leaves. Fill with shredded lamb and cover with the overhanging leaves. Press firmly to remove excess moisture and make the parcels more compact. Steam for 15 minutes before serving.

> Increase oven heat to 275°C. To prepare the **medallions of monkfish wrapped in Parma ham**, lay a piece of plastic wrap on a flat surface, then place the slices of Parma ham side-by-side to form a sheet. Place the monkfish tail in the centre of the ham and, using the plastic wrap, roll the ham around the monkfish, making the roll as tight as possible. Remove the plastic wrap and bake the roll in the oven for 8 to 10 minutes, then slice the roll into 8 medallions.

> Set each cabbage parcel on a plate and top each parcel with medallions of 2 monkfish and some fried leek.

> Warm the remaining lamb braising sauce and ladle it around the lamb parcel. Garnish the sauce with asparagus tips. (This dish may be served with risotto or purée of celery root and potatoes. Place this in a ring mould to form a base for the lamb parcel.)

Serves 4

3 lamb shanks, fat trimmed
Salt and pepper to taste
70 ml oil
150 g carrot, chopped
150 g onion, peeled and chopped
150 g celery, chopped
4 parsley stems
300 ml tomato sauce
1 L brown stock (see Basics)
400 ml red wine

8 Savoy cabbage leaves, blanched,
   refreshed, seasoned in salt and pepper,
   and central veins trimmed
4 thin slices Parma ham
240 g monkfish tail, bones removed and
   seasoned with pepper
1 leek (white part only), cut into thin strips
   and deep-fried until golden and crisp
28 asparagus tips, boiled and seasoned
   with salt and pepper

CRISP-SKIN BARRAMUNDI AND POMMES NOISETTE WITH VANILLA FOAM

Serves 4

250 g parsnips, peeled and chopped
150 g pears, cored, peeled and chopped
110 ml heavy cream
Salt and ground white pepper to taste
1 shallot, peeled and chopped
Oil for frying
5 vanilla pods
2 sprigs thyme
60 ml fish stock (see Basics)
115 g cold butter, cubed
6 to 8 medium to large red skin potatoes, peeled
1 tbsp olive oil
4 (140 g) barramundi fillets
Sea salt and ground black pepper to taste
2 tbsp clarified butter (see Basics)
12 basil leaves, deep-fried

> To prepare the **parsnip-pear purée**, boil the parsnips and pears separately in salted water until tender.
> Warm the heavy cream in a small pot. Combine the parsnips and pears in a food processor, and blend until smooth, gradually adding 50 ml of warm cream while blending. Season with salt and white pepper.
> To prepare the **vanilla foam**, sauté the shallot in oil in a small saucepot until translucent. Add the remaining cream and beans scraped from 1 vanilla pod, then reduce by half. Add the thyme and fish stock, then bring to a boil. Strain the sauce through a fine-mesh sieve and whisk in 80 g of butter cubes. Season with salt and white pepper.
> To prepare the **pommes noisette**, use a melon scoop to prepare 24 potato balls. Sauté the potato balls in

olive oil until cooked but still firm. Add the remaining cold butter and cook until the butter begins to brown. Season with salt and white pepper. Keep warm.
> To prepare the **crisp-skin barramundi**, season the barramundi fillets with sea salt and ground black pepper. Heat the clarified butter in a non-stick pan over medium-low heat and sauté the fillets, skin side down, until nearly done, then finish cooking the fish on the other side.
> Warm the vanilla sauce and use a handheld blender to process it until foamy.
> Spoon the parsnip-pear purée onto 4 plates and top with the barramundi fillets. Garnish each with fried basil leaves and a split vanilla pod. Serve with potato balls and vanilla sauce on the side.

Steamed Red Grouper with Mussels

Serves 4

12 live mussels
100 ml dry white wine
1 bay leaf
1 sprig thyme
100 g carrot, finely diced
Leek (75 g finely diced; 1 whole (white part only), cut into fine sticks and soaked in iced water for garnishing)
75 g celery, finely diced
160 g potato, finely diced
1 clove garlic, peeled and minced
2 tbsp olive oil
200 ml Pernod
300 ml fish stock (see Basics)
200 ml heavy cream
¼ tsp saffron pistils
100 g Savoy cabbage, finely shredded
Sea salt and white pepper to taste
4 (each about 120 g) red grouper fillets, skin on
4 sprigs dill

> Combine the **mussels**, wine, bay leaf and thyme in a heated sauce pot and cook covered for 5 to 6 minutes. Shake the pot once or twice. Discard any mussels that remain closed. Set both aside. Strain the liquid and set aside.
> Sauté the diced vegetables and garlic in the olive oil until fragrant, then deglaze with Pernod and cook until almost dry. Add the stock and mussel juice, and bring to a boil. Cook for 5 minutes, then add cream and saffron and continue to cook for a further 5 minutes. Add the mussels and Savoy cabbage, then remove from heat and season with salt and pepper.
> To prepare the **steamed red grouper**, season the grouper fillets with salt and pepper and steam for 8 minutes or until the fish is cooked through.
> Arrange the mussels in 4 plates and spoon the vegetable sauce over. Top each serving with a portion of fish and garnish with leek and dill.

PAN-FRIED DOVER SOLE WITH SAUTEED SCAMPI AND ASIAN MUSHROOMS

Serves 4

240 g red skin potatoes, peeled and cut
    into medium cubes
4 scampi, shells removed and
    heads reserved
150 g Japanese breadcrumbs
60 g grated Parmesan
4 (each about 400 g) Dover sole fillets
Sea salt and pepper to taste
150 g flour
2 eggs, beaten
4 tbsp clarified butter (see Basics)
30 g shimeiji mushrooms, diced
30 g shiitake mushrooms, diced
30 g oyster mushrooms, diced
30 g enoki mushrooms, diced
120 g snow peas, blanched
2 tsp finely chopped parsley
Handful of mixed herbs for garnishing
150 ml beurre blanc (see Basics)
4 tsp capers, washed

> Cook the potato cubes in salted boiling water for about 3 or 4 minutes until just tender. Drain.
> Cook the scampi heads in salted boiling water for 5 minutes. Set aside for garnishing.
> To prepare the **pan-fried Dover sole**, combine the breadcrumbs and Parmesan in a bowl and mix well. Season the sole fillets, then dredge them in flour and shake off excess. Dip them in the egg wash and coat them with the breadcrumb mixture. In a hot pan, sauté the fish with some clarified butter for 3 minutes on each side until golden.
> To prepare the **sautéed Asian mushrooms**, sauté the partially cooked potatoes and mushrooms in clarified butter in a separate pan until they begin to turn golden, then add snow peas and heat through. Season with salt, pepper and chopped parsley just before serving.
> To prepare the **sautéed scampi**, season the scampi and sauté in clarified butter until cooked through.
> Divide the potato and mushroom mixture among 4 plates, top with the fish, scampi, scampi heads and mixed herbs. Spoon the beurre blanc around and garnish the sauce with capers.

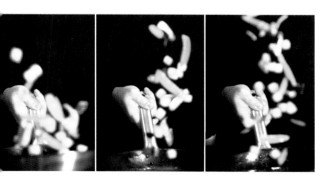

OLIVE OIL-POACHED SALMON WITH CUCUMBER VELOUTE

Serves 4

25 g onion, peeled and chopped
½ tbsp clarified butter (see Basics)
75 g cucumber, peeled and diced
1 tbsp plain flour
180 ml cold fish stock (see Basics)
2 tbsp whipping cream
Sea salt and pepper to taste
30 g baby spinach leaves
100 g watercress leaves
1 tbsp heavy cream
4 (each about 0.2 cm thick) slices peeled
  lotus root
Oil for deep-frying
1 L extra virgin olive oil
4 (each 140 g) pcs skinless salmon fillet
12 chive shoots
4 tsp salmon roe

> To prepare the cucumber velouté, sauté the onion in clarified butter in a pan until translucent. Add the cucumber and sauté briefly. Sprinkle the flour over and use a whisk to incorporate the flour thoroughly.

> While whisking, slowly add fish stock. Continue whisking until the mixture comes to a boil, then simmer for 15 minutes. If the mixture becomes too thick, add a bit of fish stock.

> Purée this mixture in a food processor until smooth and strain through a fine-mesh sieve. Return to heat and add whipping cream. Mix well and season with salt and pepper. Keep warm.

> To prepare the watercress purée, blanch the spinach and watercress leaves in salted boiling water for 10 to 15 seconds until just wilted. Refresh in an ice bath. Once cool, wring out water and purée in the food processor, slowly adding heavy cream during the process. Season with salt and pepper. Set aside.

> Deep-fry lotus root slices in oil until golden and crisp.

> To prepare the olive oil-poached salmon, heat the olive oil over low heat to 110°C. Season the salmon fillet with sea salt and pepper. Poach the salmon in the oil for 8 minutes. (When poaching, the salmon should not appear to be frying. The bubble movement should be gentle. Unlike water, oil can heat up to extreme temperatures and must be monitored to avoid excessive heating. Poaching over gentle heat will result in a delicate and tasty fillet.)

> Reheat the watercress purée and cucumber velouté.

> Remove the salmon from the oil and drain briefly before putting it on a plate.

> Spoon the sauce around the salmon and garnish the sauce with salmon roe. Top the salmon with a spoon of watercress purée and garnish with lotus root chips and chives. (You may serve this dish with horseradish or wasabi mashed potatoes.)

Sauteed Black Cod With Potato Cake And Razor Clam

Serves 4

1 sprig thyme
1 clove garlic, peeled and crushed
4 live razor or bamboo clams, cleaned
100 ml dry white wine
135 g cold butter, diced
75 ml whipping cream
Sea salt and white pepper
4 potato cakes (see Basics)
Plain flour for dredging
Clarified butter (see Basics) for cooking
4 (each about 120 to 160 g) cod fillets
A few drops of fresh lemon juice
160 g baby spinach
Oil for frying

> To prepare the **razor clams**, heat a pot large enough to hold the clams over medium-high heat. Add the thyme, garlic, clams and wine, cover and steam for 3 to 4 minutes until the clams open.
> Strain the mixture, discard the garlic and thyme, and set the juice aside. Separate the clams from their shells and set the shells aside for garnishing. Thinly slice the meaty foot of the clam on a bias to about 0.25 cm thick and discard the body.
> To prepare the **clam sauce**, combine 100 g of butter cubes, the cream and clam juice in a saucepot. Season with salt and pepper, and heat through. Use a whisk or handheld blender to process it until foamy. (Hold the blender close to the surface of the sauce so as to incorporate more air. The sauce should not be too thick, otherwise it will not become foamy. If this is the case, add a bit of water or stock and a cold cube of butter and blend again.)

> Dredge the **potato cakes** in flour and shake off excess. Add 2 tbsp of clarified butter to a hot pan and cook the potato cakes over medium heat until golden brown on both sides. Keep warm.
> To prepare the **sautéed black cod**, season the cod fillets with salt and pepper. Heat 3 tbsp of clarified butter in a non-stick pan over medium-low heat and sauté the fillets skin side down until nearly done, then finish cooking the fish on the other side.
> Heat the remaining cold butter cubes over medium-high heat until it begins to foam and turn a caramel colour. Add the clams and a few drops of lemon juice. Mix well and keep warm.
> In a pan, sauté the spinach in hot oil until just wilted. Season with salt and pepper.
> Place a potato cake on each plate, top with spinach and a cod fillet. Spoon some clam sauce on the side. Return the clams to their shells and place on the side.

Surf 'n' turf with sweet potato agnolotti

Serves 4

400 g sweet potatoes, peeled and boiled
2 eggs
60 ml clarified butter, warmed (see Basics)
Salt and pepper to taste
330 ml heavy cream (whip 80 ml until stiff
   enough to form a peak)
Plain flour for dusting
1 sheet (300 g) pasta dough (see Basics)
Olive oil for frying

1 shallot, peeled and chopped
1 clove garlic, peeled and crushed
50 ml dry white wine
8 sprigs rosemary
75 g Roquefort cheese
1 L brown stock (see Basics)
4 prawns, shells removed
4 slices streaky bacon
4 beef fillets

> To prepare the **sweet potato agnolotti**, purée the sweet potatoes in a food processor until smooth. Whisk 1 egg yolk vigorously until it doubles in volume and turns pale yellow, then slowly add the clarified butter in a steady stream while whisking. If necessary, add 1 tbsp of hot water to dilute the mixture. Fold this into the sweet potato purée, season with salt and pepper, then fold in the whipped cream.

> Dust a flat surface with flour, then lay a sheet of pasta dough on it. Fill a pastry bag with the sweet potato purée, then pipe 28 balls (each about 1.5 cm in diameter) in a straight line (keeping them 2 cm apart) just below the middle of the pasta sheet.

> Beat the other egg with 1 tsp of water, then brush the top half of the pasta sheet with it. Fold the bottom half of the pasta over the filling and use your fingers to crimp the pasta in the spaces between. Using a pasta cutter, slowly cut along the length of the pasta, then cut between the pockets.

> In a pot, sauté the shallot and garlic in oil until fragrant. Deglaze with wine and cook until dry. Add the heavy cream and 4 rosemary sprigs and reduce heat to a simmer. Slowly reduce the mixture until thick. Strain and mix in Roquefort cheese. Keep warm.

> Over medium to high heat, reduce the brown stock to the consistency of a rich sauce. Strain and keep warm.

> Wrap each **prawn** with a slice of bacon and secure with a bamboo skewer. Sauté the prawns in olive oil for 3 minutes on each side.

> Preheat oven to 275°C. Season the **beef** with salt and pepper, then sear it on all sides in a pan heated with oil. Finish cooking in the oven to desired doneness. Allow to rest for 5 minutes before serving.

> Cook the pasta in salted boiling water for 2 minutes, then add it to the Roquefort cream sauce.

> Ladle brown sauce on 4 plates, spoon some pasta over and top with a beef fillet and prawn. Garnish with a rosemary sprig.

Steamed Clams in Vegetable Nage Scented with Anise and Orange

Serves 6 to 8

25 g mint leaves
25 g basil leaves
25 g parsley leaves
1 clove garlic, peeled and minced
1 ½ tbsp capers
2 anchovy fillets
¼ tsp Dijon mustard
¼ tsp sea salt
¼ tsp sugar
½ tbsp black peppercorns
¼ tbsp red pepper flakes
90 ml olive oil
100 ml mayonnaise
1 fennel, cut into thin sticks
2 carrots, cut into thin sticks
3 leeks (white part only), cut into thin sticks
1.5 L fish stock (see Basics)
½ tsp saffron pistils
1 bay leaf
1 sprig dried thyme
3 star anise pods
Zest from ½ orange, cut into thin sticks
60 ml Pernod
5 tomatoes, peeled and cut into thin strips
100 small or medium clams
6 to 8 pcs focaccia, cut into preferred shape

> To prepare **salsa verde aioli**, purée the herbs, garlic, capers, anchovies, mustard, salt and peppers in a food processor, then set on low speed and slowly incorporate 60 ml of olive oil until well mixed. Add the mayonnaise and blend well. Adjust seasoning to taste.
> To prepare the **vegetable nage**, heat the remaining oil in a pot, add the fennel, carrots and leeks and sauté until translucent. Add the stock and bring to a boil, then reduce heat and add all the remaining ingredients, except the tomatoes, clams and bread, and simmer for 8 minutes.
> Add the tomatoes and **clams**, cover and steam for 4 minutes or until the clams open. Adjust seasoning to taste and discard any unopened clams.
> Toast the bread and spread generously with the salsa verde aioli.
> Divide the clams among 6 to 8 serving bowls, ladle the nage and vegetables over and serve warm with toast on the side.

HERB-CRUSTED SCALLOPS AND SPINACH TAGLIATELLE WITH SORREL VELOUTE

Serves 4

125 g breadcrumbs
50 g butter
2 egg whites
1 tsp lemon juice
Zest from 1 lemon, blanched and minced
12 g chervil leaves
40 g parsley leaves
10 g tarragon leaves
Salt and pepper to taste
300 ml whipping cream
2 shallots, peeled and minced
4 tbsp unsalted butter
2 tbsp plain flour, sifted
1 tbsp clarified butter (see Basics)
500 ml hot fish stock (see Basics)
100 g sorrel leaves, blanched, refreshed
    and chopped
16 large scallops
Olive oil for frying
Spinach tagliatelle (see Basics)
2 tsp minced garlic
4 tbsp Parmesan shavings
A few chive sticks

> To prepare the **herb crust**, blend the breadcrumbs, butter, egg whites, lemon juice and zest, herbs, salt and pepper in a food processor until just mixed. Knead into a dough by hand and cut into 3 equal parts. Spread plastic wrap on a flat surface and place 1 part on it. Flatten with your palm then cover with plastic. Roll out the dough evenly (about 0.3 cm thick). Repeat with the remaining dough and freeze. Cut 16 discs using a 2.5-cm diameter cookie cutter.
> To prepare the **sorrel velouté**, reduce the cream by half and set aside. Mix the clarified butter and flour to make roux. Sauté the shallots in butter until translucent. Add the roux and stock and whisk until smooth. Bring to a boil, then simmer for 10 minutes. Add the sorrel leaves and cream. Mix well. Season.
> Preheat oven to 200°C. Season the **scallops** and pan-fry each side for 45 seconds. Top with herb discs and bake for 4 to 6 minutes until golden.
> Cook the **spinach tagliatelle** in salted boiling water for 2 to 3 minutes until al dente. Sauté the garlic in oil until fragrant. Add the pasta and heat through.
> Spoon sauce on plates. Top with scallops and pasta. Garnish with Parmesan shavings and chives.

Warm Chocolate Truffle Cake with Tonka Bean and Nut Ice Cream

Serves 8 to 10

150 g dark chocolate, chopped
135 g butter
6 eggs
75 g sugar
60 g all purpose flour, sieved
Icing sugar for dusting
8 to 10 scoops tonka bean and nut ice cream (see Basics)
30 raspberries
4 or 5 tbsp chocolate sauce

> Preheat oven to 190°C and grease 8 to 10 cupcake or soufflé moulds with butter, then line them with greaseproof paper.
> To prepare the **warm chocolate truffle cake**, combine chocolate and butter in a heatproof mixing bowl and melt over double boiler.
> In a separate mixing bowl, whisk the eggs and sugar until well incorporated then add to the chocolate mixture and mix well. Fold in the flour gradually until well incorporated.
> Fill 80 per cent of each mould with the batter and bake in the oven for 8 to 12 minutes until the outer edges of the cakes are cooked but the centres are still liquid.
> Gently remove the cakes from their moulds to serving plates, taking care not to puncture them. Dust the cakes with icing sugar. Place a scoop of **tonka bean and nut ice cream** beside each cake and garnish with raspberries and chocolate sauce.

SOY PANNA COTTA WITH RHUBARB COMPOTE

Serves 6

90 ml milk
350 ml soy milk
150 ml heavy cream
190 g sugar
4½ sheets gelatine, soaked in ice
  water until soft then drained
1 vanilla pod
150 ml sugar syrup (see Basics)
3 stalks fresh rhubarb, peel
  removed and reserved, flesh
  finely diced
Puff pastry (see Basics)
1 egg, beaten
6 gooseberries

> To prepare the **panna cotta**, combine the milk, soy milk, heavy cream and 90 g of sugar in a pot and simmer until the sugar is dissolved. Add the gelatine, bring to a boil, then remove from heat and set aside.

> Combine the remaining sugar with 2 tbsp of water in a sauce pot and stir over medium heat until the sugar starts to melt. When the sugar begins to boil, do not stir but gently swirl the pan occasionally until it turns a deep caramel colour. Place the bottom of the pot in an ice bath to stop the caramel from burning. Divide the caramel among 6 round moulds, top with the panna cotta mix and chill for 4 hours.

> To prepare the **rhubarb compôte**, split the vanilla pod in half, lengthwise, and scrape out the seeds. Combine both the seeds and pod with the syrup and rhubarb peel in a pot and bring to a boil. Lower heat to a simmer and reduce the liquid by a third.

Strain the syrup, return it to the pot and add the rhubarb flesh. Bring the mixture to a boil, then simmer until the rhubarb is soft and has taken on the consistency of compôte.

> Preheat oven to 180°C. Roll out the pastry dough evenly (about 0.3 cm thick), then use a cookie cutter to cut circles just larger than the base of the moulds.

> Prick the dough with a fork, place on a baking tray, and cover with greaseproof paper. Weigh it down with another tray and bake in the oven for 10 minutes. Remove from heat and brush with the beaten egg then bake for a further 5 minutes at 130°C.

> Dip the panna cotta moulds in hot water until the panna cotta can be removed from the mould easily.

> Place a pastry dough cookie on a plate and top with a serving of panna cotta. Spoon some rhubarb compôte on the side and garnish with a gooseberry.

CHOCOLATE TART WITH CREME ANGLAISE

Serves 8

60 g castor sugar
90 g butter (at room temperature)
Seeds from 1 vanilla pod
3 eggs, beaten
170 g plain flour, sifted
Pinch of salt
1 egg yolk beaten with 2 tsp water
   for egg wash
50 ml milk
250 ml whipping cream
400 g quality unsweetened dark
   chocolate (Valrhona, Barry
   Callebaut or Lindt), chopped
100 ml strong coffee, warm
100 ml sugar syrup (see Basics)
Zest from 2 grapefruit
300 ml crème anglaise (see Basics)
200 ml sweetened whipped cream
8 tuiles (see Basics)

> To prepare the **chocolate tart**, use an electric mixer to mix the sugar and butter until smooth but not fluffy.
> Mix in the vanilla seeds, then set the mixer on the lowest speed and blend in 1 beaten egg. Gradually incorporate the flour and salt. When a crumbly dough is formed, stop the mixer. Knead the dough by hand on a floured surface to get a smooth ball. Cover with plastic wrap and rest for 30 minutes.
> Preheat oven to 180°C. Roll out the pastry dough evenly (about 3 cm thick). It should be able to cover a 21-cm-diameter pie tin (with removable base) and have its sides hanging over the rim. Press the pastry evenly into the tin, prick the base with a fork and mend any tears (do not trim the sides). Cover the dough with baking paper and weigh it down with some beans. Chill for 10 minutes, then bake (with paper and beans) for 10 minutes.

> Remove from heat and remove the paper and beans. Trim the sides and bake for a further 5 minutes until it starts to colour. Lower oven temperature to 130°C. Brush the dough with egg wash and bake for 5 more minutes. Remove from heat and set aside.
> Increase oven temperature to 140°C. Bring the milk and cream to a boil then pour over the chocolate and coffee and mix well. Mix in 2 beaten eggs then strain through a fine-mesh sieve and pour into the baked pie crust. Bake for 25 minutes or until it starts to set. Remove from heat and leave in a warm place for 30 minutes. When cool, unmould the tart.
> To prepare the **grapefruit zest confit**, bring the syrup to a boil and add the grapefruit zest. Remove from heat and let the zest cool in the syrup.
> Serve the tart with the grapefruit zest confit, **crème anglaise**, sweetened whipped cream and tuiles.

RICE PUDDING MILLE FEUILLE WITH POACHED PEAR

Serves 4

50 g glutinous rice, rinsed
60 ml milk
60 ml whipping cream
½ vanilla pod
75 g castor sugar
1 egg yolk
8 (40-by-50-cm) sheets filo pastry
 (see Basics)
150 g tinned pear, drained
5 cinnamon sticks
1 clove
3 whole allspice berries
600 ml dry white wine
200 g sugar
4 whole pears, peeled, with stems intact
Icing sugar for dusting

> To prepare the **rice pudding**, split the vanilla pod in half, lengthwise, and scrape out the seeds. Combine the pod, seeds, rice, milk and cream in a pot and simmer for 15 to 20 minutes until the rice is just cooked. Stir to prevent burning.

> Whisk 25 g of castor sugar with the egg yolk until the mixture turns pale yellow. Gradually add some cooked rice to warm the egg mixture up, then mix this with the rest of the rice. Cook over low heat, stirring constantly until the mixture is thick. Remove from heat and set aside. Stir regularly to prevent a layer from forming on the pudding surface.

> Preheat oven to 180°C. Purée the pear and remaining castor sugar in a food processor until smooth. Place 1 filo sheet on a flat working surface and spread a thin layer of pear purée over. Cover with another sheet of filo and repeat process twice more, finishing with a 4th sheet of filo on the top. Prepare 1 more set with the other 4 filo sheets. Cut them into 9-by-5-cm rectangles (allocate 4 rectangles per serving) and bake (flatten rectangles with a heavy oven-proof pan while baking) for 10 to 12 minutes until golden.

> To prepare the **poached pears**, mix 1 cinnamon stick, clove, allspice berries, wine and sugar in a pot and bring to a boil. Stir until the sugar dissolves. Add the pears and simmer for 12 minutes, then remove from heat and leave the pears to infuse for 1 hour. Set the pears aside and return the liquid to the heat and reduce until it reaches a syrup-like consistency.

> To prepare the **mille feuille**, spread a filo crisp with a thin layer of rice pudding. Cover with another crisp and repeat process twice more. Finish with a 4th crisp on top. Prepare 4 sets. Dust with icing sugar.

> Serve the mille feuille with a poached pear drizzled with poaching syrup. Garnish with cinnamon sticks.

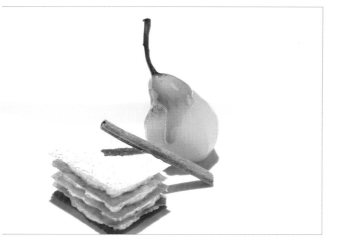

MANGO SOUP WITH POMELO AND SOURSOP SORBET

> To prepare the **mango soup**, purée the mango, milk, syrup, 100 ml of water and orange juice in a food processor until smooth, then pass the mixture through a fine-mesh sieve. Keep refrigerated until required.
> To prepare the **beignets**, dissolve the yeast in 95 ml of warm water. Combine this with the egg, evaporated milk, sugar and salt in the bowl of a mixer and use the dough hook attachment to blend well. Add half the flour and keep mixing until smooth. Add the shortening and remaining flour and continue working the dough with the mixer until well mixed.
> Using your hands, knead the dough on a floured surface for about 5 minutes or until smooth. Keep chilled and covered for 1 hour, then roll out the dough evenly (about 0.3 cm thick). Cut into batons or desired shape and keep chilled until required.
> Deep-fry the dough in hot oil until golden. Remove from oil with a strainer and soak up excess oil with kitchen paper. Dust generously with icing sugar.
> Divide the chilled mango purée into bowls or glasses and add the **pomelo** sacs. Top with **soursop sorbet** and serve with a beignet on the side.

Serves 6 to 8

400 g very ripe mango, peeled, pitted
 and chopped
400 ml milk
100 ml sugar syrup (see Basics)
195 ml water
100 ml orange juice
6 g active dry yeast
1 egg
70 ml evaporated milk
30 g sugar
Pinch of salt
250 g flour, sifted
15 g shortening
Oil for deep-frying
Icing sugar to taste
6 to 8 tbsp pomelo sacs
6 to 8 scoops soursop sorbet (see Basics)

BASICS AND GLOSSARY

ALLSPICE

> A Caribbean spice with a mildly sweet flavour, reminiscent of cinnamon, cloves and nutmeg. Available in both whole berry and ground form.

BEURRE BLANC   Makes 200 ml

1 shallot, peeled and minced
2 tsp oil for frying
50 ml dry white wine
1 tsp cider vinegar
20 ml lemon juice
50 ml heavy cream
140 g butter, diced
Salt and white pepper to taste

> Sauté the shallots in oil until translucent, then deglaze with white wine, vinegar and lemon juice. Reduce until dry, then add the cream and reduce by half.
> Reduce heat and slowly whisk in 1 or 2 cubes of butter at a time. Do not let the sauce boil. Move the pot away from the heat whenever necessary. When all the butter has been incorporated, remove from heat and season to taste.

BRIOCHE

> Soft, light-textured French bread prepared with eggs, butter, flour and yeast.

BROWN STOCK   Makes 1 L

1 kg veal or lamb bones
1.5 L cold water

2 tbsp oil
60 g onion
30 g celery
30 g carrot
1 tbsp tomato paste
1 sprig parsley
1 clove garlic
1 bay leaf
3 peppercorns, crushed

> Preheat oven to 200°C. Roast the veal bones in the oven until well browned.
> Place the bones in a pot and cover them with cold water. Bring to a boil, then simmer for 5 hours and skim the surface regularly.
> In the roasting pan used for the bones, heat the oil, add the onion, celery and carrot, and cook until caramelised. Add tomato paste, and when it begins to caramelise, deglaze with some water.
> Using a wooden spoon, scrape the pan for the scraps left from roasting the bones. Add these, along with the parsley, garlic, bay leaf and peppercorns to the stock. Simmer for 1 hour, then strain to use.

CIABATTA

> Ciabatta means 'slipper' in Italian, and it refers to the flat, rectangular, slipper-shaped Italian bread with a thick crust used for sandwiches.

CEVICHE

> Fish or seafood that has been cured with a citric marinade. It is the national dish of Peru, and is also popular throughout Latin America.

Chicken Stock Makes 1 L

1 kg chicken bones, chopped
1.5 L cold water
60 g onion, peeled and chopped
30 g celery, chopped
30 g carrot, chopped
2 bay leaves
25 g parsley stems
1 tbsp black peppercorns, crushed
4 cloves garlic, peeled and crushed

> Rinse the chopped chicken bones with cold water.
> Combine the bones and water in a pot and bring to a boil, then reduce heat and simmer for 3 hours, skimming the surface regularly.
> Add the remaining ingredients and keep simmering for a further 1 hour.
> Strain stock before using. If you are not using the stock immediately, leave at room temperature to cool then keep frozen until required.

Chocolate Ice Cream Makes 3 L

480 ml milk
480 ml heavy cream
1 vanilla pod (optional)
8 egg yolks
225 g sugar
150 g cocoa powder

> Combine the milk and cream in a pot and bring to a slow simmer.
> Slit the vanilla pod lengthwise and scrape out the seeds. Add the vanilla pod and seeds to the milk mixture and set aside to infuse for 10 minutes.
> Whisk the egg yolks and sugar in a mixing bowl vigorously until it turns pale yellow and smooth.

> Temper the egg mixture by adding 1 ladleful of the warm milk mixture at a time and mixing well. Repeat this step 3 or 4 times until the temperature of the egg mixture equalises with that of the warm milk mixture (this process prevents the eggs from curdling once added to the warm milk).
> Add the tempered egg mixture to the remaining milk mixture in the pot and cook over low heat, stirring constantly with a wooden spoon until the mixture thickens.
> Add the cocoa powder and mix well.
> Remove the vanilla pod and cool the mixture by placing the pot in an ice bath.
> Process the mixture in an ice cream machine following the manufacturer's instructions. Keep frozen until required.

Clarified Butter

> Butter is clarified by the removal of the milk solids and water from the fat. This will result in a golden liquid with hints of butter that will not burn because it has a much higher smoking point.
> Clarified butter is used to prepare dishes which require a buttery flavour but must be cooked over moderately high heat. It can be made in large quantities, and kept refrigerated for several weeks or frozen until required.
> To make clarified butter, slowly melt unsalted butter in a pan over gentle heat, skimming away any foam that rises to the top. Once the butter stops foaming, remove the pan from the heat and allow the milk solids to settle, then pour the clear golden clarified butter into a separate container and discard the milk solids and water left in the pan.

CORN MUFFINS Makes 12

225 g plain flour
1½ tsp baking powder
75 g shortening
150 g sugar
Salt to taste
2 eggs
225 ml milk
150 g corn meal (polenta)

> Preheat oven to 220°C.
> Sift the flour and baking powder together.
> In a mixing bowl, thoroughly mix the shortening, sugar and salt. Gradually whisk in the eggs, scraping the sides when necessary. Gradually whisk in the milk, followed by the corn meal. Blend well. Fold in the flour and mix until smooth. Divide the batter into greased or paper-lined muffin tins and bake in the oven for 20 minutes or until golden brown.

CRAYFISH SAUCE Makes 1 L

80 g fennel, chopped
40 g onion, peeled and chopped
40 g celery, chopped
25 g leek, chopped
40 g carrot, chopped
60 ml clarified butter
700 g crayfish shells, chopped
120 ml Cognac
40 g tomato paste
2 L light fish stock
10 g parsley stems
1 bay leaf
60 ml heavy cream
Salt and pepper to taste

> Sweat the fennel, onion, celery, leek and carrot in clarified butter until they start to brown. Add the crayfish shells and sauté until they start to brown.

Deglaze with Cognac and cook until almost dry.
> Add the tomato paste and cook for 30 seconds. Add the fish stock, parsley stems and bay leaf, bring to a boil, then simmer for 30 minutes.
> Remove from heat and strain through a fine-mesh sieve or cheesecloth. Return to heat and reduce until a quarter is left.
> Add the cream and return to a boil, whisking constantly. Season with salt and pepper.

CREAM

> Heavy cream, also called heavy whipping cream, has between 36 and 40 per cent butterfat, and doubles its volume when whipped. Whipping cream, on the other hand, has a lower butterfat content of 30 per cent, and is more suitable for piping.

CREME ANGLAISE Makes 250 ml

½ vanilla pod
170 ml milk
2 egg yolks
40 g sugar

> Split the vanilla pod in half, lengthwise, and combine with the milk in a pot. Bring to a simmer.
> Whisk the sugar with the egg yolks until smooth and pale yellow. Temper this mixture by mixing in a little hot milk, then adding a little of this to the hot milk. Repeat this 3 or 4 times until the temperatures of both mixtures equalise (this prevents the eggs from curdling when added to the hot milk), then mix both together. Cook over low heat, stirring constantly with a wooden spoon, until the mixture thickens.
> Remove vanilla pod and cool by placing the pot in an ice bath. Keep refrigerated until required.

Creme fraiche

> Similar to sour cream but with higher butterfat content, this has a slightly tangy and nutty flavour, and rich, velvety texture. It is available in varying thicknesses and can be boiled without curdling. Usually whipped and used as a topping for fresh fruit or desserts.

Filo pastry

> Also spelled as 'phyllo', this Greek pastry is characteristically paper-thin, and readily available in supermarkets. Defrost frozen filo by leaving the unopened package in the refrigerator overnight rather than at room temperature or the sheets will stick. It also dries quickly once exposed to air.

Fish stock   Makes 1 L

    1 kg white fish bones, blanched
    1 L cold water
    60 g onion, peeled and chopped
    30 g celery, chopped
    30 g carrot, chopped
    250 ml dry white wine
    1 bay leaf
    1 parsley stem
    3 black peppercorns, crushed
    1 clove garlic, peeled and crushed

> Blanch the fish bones in a pot of boiling water for 3 minutes and discard the water, leaving the bones in the pot. Add all the remaining ingredients and bring to a boil, then simmer for 45 minutes and skim the surface regularly.
> Strain stock before using. If you are not using the stock immediately, leave to cool then keep frozen until required.

Foccacia

> Italian flat bread flavoured with olive oil, salt, herbs and assorted toppings. This is also used to make panini, a layered Italian sandwich.

Foie gras

> In French 'foie gras' means 'fat liver' and refers to the liver of a fattened goose or duck.

Gravlax

> A Swedish speciality of fresh salmon fillets cured with a mixture of salt, sugar, dill and various spices. It is sliced thinly and eaten with dark bread, or served as part of a smörgåsbord with dill-mustard sauce.

Jicama

> A tuber with a crisp texture somewhat between an apple and a water chestnut. Can be served raw as a snack, or lightly roasted.

Mignonette

> A classic dressing or dip for oysters, made from white wine, sherry vinegar, shallots, and pepper.

Mille feuille

> French for 'a thousand leaves', this is a classic French dessert made with layers of crisp puff pastry spread with pastry cream, custard, jam or fruit purée.

Orange marmalade   Serves 4

150 g orange segments, seeds and pith removed
1 slice orange zest
2 tsp lemon juice
1½ tbsp brown sugar

> Combine all the ingredients in a small pot and bring to a slow boil. Keep cooking until a jam-like consistency is reached. The marmalade will become thicker at room temperature.

Pancetta

> Pork that has been dried and cured, similar to bacon. Added to pasta sauces or over pizzas.

Parma ham

> Pepper-flavoured raw ham from the Parma district in Italy, that has been dried and cured.

Pasta dough   Makes 600 g

510 g plain flour
3 g salt
3 egg whites
4 egg yolks
50 ml olive oil

> Combine all the ingredients in an electric mixer attached with a dough hook and blend well. (Or you may place the flour in a mound, make a well in the centre and add the salt, eggs and oil. Use a fork to beat the egg mixture, slowly incorporating the flour until most of it has been mixed in.)
> Knead into a dough with your hands on a floured surface until light and elastic.

> Let it rest in an oiled and covered bowl for 15 minutes before rolling it out with a pasta machine and cutting into desired shape.

Pernod

> A brand of liqueur popular in France. It is colourless with a sharp aniseed flavour, and turns cloudy when mixed with water.

Potato cakes   Serves 4

2 large russet or Idaho potatoes, rinsed and rubbed with salt
120 g cod scraps, diced and seasoned with salt and pepper
¼ onion, peeled and coarsely diced
2.5 cm piece of carrot, coarsely diced
2.5 cm piece of celery, coarsely diced
½ clove garlic, peeled and crushed
1 sprig thyme
50 ml water
2 egg whites, lightly beaten
1½ tbsp potato flour
1 tbsp finely chopped chives
Salt and pepper to taste

> Preheat oven to 180°C. Bake the potatoes for 30 to 40 minutes until cooked but still firm in the centre.
> Simmer the cod scraps with the onion, carrot, celery, garlic, thyme and water in a covered pot for 8 minutes until the cod is just cooked. Remove the cod and rinse it under cold running water.
> Peel the potatoes and remove blemishes. Grate them with a cheese grater, then mix with the egg whites, potato flour, chives and cod scraps. Season to taste.
> Roll the potato in greaseproof paper into a 6-cm-long cylinder. Secure both ends by twisting them as tightly as possible in opposite directions. Chill the log in the freezer until firm then slice into 1.5-cm-thick cakes.

Puff Pastry Makes 3.25 kg

225 g cake flour
900 g bread flour
1.12 kg butter
600 ml water
½ tsp salt

> Sift the cake and bread flour together. Set a fifth of this aside.
> Rub 120 g of butter into the remaining flour mixture. Add water and salt, then knead into a smooth dough. Refrigerate.
> Combine the remaining butter with the reserved flour and knead until smooth.
> Roll out the dough evenly into a 45-by-45-cm square. Cool it in the refrigerator slightly but do not allow the butter to get firm and brittle.
> Roll out the first piece of dough into a 45-by-60-cm rectangle. Place the 45-by-45-cm piece of dough on one end of the rectangular piece, leaving a third of it exposed. Fold the exposed portion over the square, then fold the other end of the dough over the first fold. Roll this out to a 45-by-45-cm square, rotate it by 90° and let it rest for 20 minutes.
> Fold both ends of the dough towards the centre, then roll out the dough to a 45-by-45-cm square, rotate it by 90° and let it rest for 20 minutes.
> Repeat this step 3 more times.
> Roll out the dough evenly (0.3 or 0.4 cm thick), cut into desired portion and keep frozen until required.

Rhubarb

> Rhubarb is a vegetable whose stems are most commonly sweetened with sugar to minimise their extreme tartness and used to make pies, tarts, puddings, breads, jams and refreshing drinks.

Shiso cress

> Also known as perilla leaf, this herb is rich in flavour and the leaves are commonly used as a garnish.

Shucking oysters

> Scrub the oysters under running water to remove all dirt. Discard any oysters that are open, even those that are slightly open (this means that they are dead and not suitable for consumption).
> To protect your hands, use a dish towel to hold the oyster flat side facing up and insert an oyster knife into an opening close to the hinge.
> Pry the oyster open by twisting the knife and moving it clockwise and counter clockwise (rather than up and down because this action will break the knife).
> Once the shells are open, carefully slice through the conductor muscle which holds the 2 shells together, by pressing your knife firmly against the inner part of the top shell. Repeat this process with the conductor muscle of the bottom shell.

Soursop sorbet Makes 1 L

200 ml water
50 g sugar
650 g soursop purée
1 egg white, whipped into soft peaks
1 tbsp lime juice

> Combine the water and sugar in a pot and heat until the sugar dissolves completely. Cool by placing the pot in an ice bath.
> Combine this with the remaining ingredients. Mix well. Process this in an ice cream machine following the manufacturer's instructions for making a sorbet.

Spinach Tagliatelle Serves 4

40 g spinach leaves
260 g plain flour, sifted
1 egg
1 egg yolk
30 ml olive oil
2 g salt

> Blanch the spinach in boiling water then refresh in iced water. Purée the spinach with 25 ml of the blanching water in a food processor.
> Combine all the ingredients in an electric mixer attached with a dough hook and blend well. (Or you may place the flour in a mound on a clean surface, make a well in the centre and add the egg, yolk, spinach, oil and salt. Use a fork to beat the egg mixture, slowly incorporating the flour until most of it has been mixed in.) Knead into a dough with your hands on a floured surface until tight and elastic.
> Let it rest in an oiled and covered bowl for 15 minutes before rolling it out with a pasta machine and cutting into 0.5-cm wide strips.

Sugar syrup Makes 250 ml

200 ml water
50 g sugar

> Combine the water and sugar in a pot and heat until the sugar dissolves completely.

Tatsoi leaf

> Also called 'Chinese flat cabbage', this is a vegetable with dark green, spoon-shaped leaves and a light cabbage taste. Recommended stir-fried or in salads and soups.

Tonka bean

> Black, nut-like seeds of a tall South American tree used for its aromatic properties in perfumes and medicines as well as a substitute for vanilla. Also called 'coumara nut'.

Tonka bean and nut ice cream
Makes 3 L

480 ml milk
480 ml heavy cream
5 tonka beans
8 egg yolks
225 g sugar
150 g raisins, chopped
200 g toasted nuts, chopped

> Combine the milk and cream in a pot and bring to a slow simmer. Add the tonka beans to the milk mixture and set aside to infuse for 10 minutes.
> Combine the egg yolks and sugar in a mixing bowl and whisk vigorously until it becomes pale yellow and smooth.
> Temper the mixture by adding 1 ladleful of the warm milk mixture at a time and mixing well. Repeat this step 3 or 4 times until the temperature of the egg mixture equalises with that of the warm milk mixture (this process prevents the eggs from curdling once added to the warm milk).
> Add the tempered egg mixture to the remaining milk mixture in the pot and cook over low heat, stirring constantly with a wooden spoon until the mixture thickens. Cool the mixture by placing the pot in an ice bath.
> Add the chopped raisins and nuts and mix well.
> Process the mixture in an ice cream machine following the manufacturer's instructions.

Tuiles Makes 18 to 24

50 g plain flour, sifted
50 g castor sugar
50 g egg white
50 g butter, melted
Drop of vanilla essence

> Preheat oven to 200°C.
> Combine the flour and sugar in the bowl of an electric mixer. With the mixer running slowly, incorporate the egg whites, melted butter and vanilla essence until well mixed.
> Using a stencil [make your own stencil by drawing desired shape on a heavy plastic sheet (such as the plastic cover of a document folder) and cutting out the shape with scissors or a sharp knife] to create desired shape, spread a thin and even layer of batter on a sheet of greaseproof paper, silicone baking mat or baking tray.
> Bake for 5 to 8 minutes or until golden.

Vanilla

> One of the world's most expensive spices, vanilla is native to Mexico. Its highly aromatic flavour is derived from the dark brown, slender and pleated seed pod or 'bean' of the plant. The best vanilla comes from Mexico and Madagascar.

Vanilla ice cream Makes 3 L

480 ml milk
480 ml heavy cream
1 vanilla pod
8 egg yolks
225 g sugar

> Combine the milk and cream in a pot and bring to a slow simmer.
> Slit the vanilla pod lengthwise and scrape out the seeds. Add the pod and seeds to the milk mixture and infuse for 10 minutes.
> Combine the egg yolks and sugar in a mixing bowl and whisk vigorously until it becomes pale yellow and smooth.
> Temper the mixture by adding 1 ladleful of the warm milk mixture at a time and mixing well. Repeat this step 3 or 4 times until the temperature of the egg mixture equalises with that of the warm milk mixture (this process prevents the eggs from curdling once added to the warm milk).
> Add the tempered egg mixture to the remaining milk mixture in the pot and cook over low heat, stirring constantly with a wooden spoon until the mixture thickens.
> Remove the vanilla pod and cool the mixture by placing the pot in an ice bath.
> Process the mixture in an ice cream machine following the manufacturer's instructions.

Wasabi

> Wasabi is Japanese horseradish with a fiery taste that quickly dissipates in the mouth and is typically used as a condiment for sashimi and sushi. Fresh wasabi is a highly sought-after and very expensive ingredient served mainly in the top restaurants and sushi bars of Japan. The green root vegetable, when grated into a paste, is a lot more delicate in flavour than the commonly available wasabi paste and powder, which contain little or no real wasabi and derive their fiery flavour from mustard powder and green hue from artificial food colouring.

CHAMPAGNE
DUVAL-LEROY